Raise Your Voice

You may be thinking that the insiders have the game rigged and your voice will never be heard. Not so. You are reading this book because we started asking questions, finding answers, and talking to people. The lesson we learned is that every voice in the market is important and needs to be heard.

Stay Informed

The market is dynamic. Investors need to keep up to be aware of the trading games that the exchanges and HFTs play. Many trade magazines and blogs offer detailed insight, and they are free. For example:

- **Advanced Trading:** www.advancedtrading.com
- **FT Trading Room:** www.ft.com/intl/trading-room
- **Securities Technology Monitor:** www.securitiestechnologymonitor.com
- **Tabb Forum:** www.tabbforum.com
- **Themis Trading Blog:** blog.themistrading.com
- **Zero Hedge:** www.zerohedge.com
- **Traders Magazine:** www.tradersmagazine.com

Comment

Investors should comment about proposals that they think are unfair. Before new regulations or exchange rules are implemented, there is a public comment period. Look for these proposals on the SEC's website at www.sec.gov and submit an email. Click the Proposed Rules tab and pay particular attention to the "SRO Rulemaking" section.

Day Trading for the Complete Beginner
How to get Financial Freedom from Day Trading
By Joseph Richards
Copyright 2015

If you enjoyed learning the information in this book... you may also be interested in...

These other titles by Joseph Richards

Day Trading Stocks Online using Supply and Demand
12 Characteristics of Highly Successful Day Traders
Brand New Forex Day Traders Bible Book
Forex, Futures and Stocks Day Trading with a Rule Based Plan
How to not make Costly Mistakes Day Trading Forex
Supply & Demand Day Trading for Futures

If you have been helped by purchasing this book please take a minute by letting me know how it helped you by leaving a review on the site where you purchased this book.

I am always interested to know how my readers are doing and what successes they are having in the markets.

Wishing you a profitable day!

Joseph Richards

Who I wrote this book for

This book is written for all of the up and coming aspiring day traders and investors who are trying to figure out if this business is for them or not. By the time you are reading the first few pages of this book you will know what is in store for you in the business of making money with money and if you want to do it or not.

Investing and trading is the best business in the world as far as I am concerned. It is the only business I know of where you can be at the beach on a beautiful sunny day or scuba diving or flying to Europe for the weekend to meet up with friends and still be making money the whole time you're doing it.

You don't need a job you need an income and trading is the only business I know of where you can be anywhere in the world you choose to be day or night and having the chance to make money. Isn't that the type of business you would like to be in? For me it was a no brainer decision. Now I can do my business anywhere in the world I wish to be and know that my business is taking care of itself because I have my positions being monitored in the live market by my rule based plan.

No other business in the world other than trading allows you to work at your own pace and make an unlimited amount of money. A brand new trader with no experience can read this book and depending on how fast they can grasp the concepts and learn them can be making an income for themselves in as little as 30 days to 6 months.

Learning the trading business is not as hard as one would imagine as long as you are learning it the right way the first time from the first day. This book and the information it provides to brand new investors and traders is like having the keys to your mansion, Ferrari and super yacht handed to you all at the same time. You can certainly have all of those things and more if you just take your time and go slow and logically think through what this book is telling you to do.

There is a certain progression of steps that every new equities trader (or any trader) must follow to become a consistently profitable professional trader. There are absolutely no short cuts. Should any brand new trader decide to try to side step any part of the proper education and training and try to go into the live markets before you have become consistent on a demo account for however long it takes, you stand the chance of your money train going wildly off the tracks and possibly losing *all* of your capital.

With some good planning and the right education and training from the very start a new investor and trader can get up to speed fairly quickly and then it is a matter of polishing ones skills and plan. Once they are confident in their skills and their plan is solid they should have no problems going into the live market and becoming a successful market participant.

The most important thing about market education is learning it the right way from the beginning and *not* making the mistakes that other people are making. Don't become one of the sheeple of the herd. If you learn what *not* to do right from the very start, you will already have an edge over the others who did not take the time to educate themselves properly—this is whom you can actually make money from in the markets once you can see their fear and greed.

I wrote this book for all the new and upcoming aspiring day traders, swing traders and investors who are coming into the business and have zero or very limited knowledge so they won't have to waste valuable learning time and money to figure out only the most important things to know on their own.

I know you have probably read this before however I feel I owe you the best information so I will say it again right here. Investing and trading is not a get rich quick business.

While the market *is* like a big ATM that is open 24 hours a day if you don't have the right PIN# *your* money will get sucked *into it*. Learning to trade on demo is not some video game. If you are going to make the decision to learn this business than you had be learn it the right way the first time from the first day.

Make no mistake this is a dead serious business and you should treat that way. You as a retail investor or trader have a limited chance of having a positive outcome in the live market against the best market participants in the world not to mention having to try to make money from the machines. It is said that 70% of the market making is done by super computers now. You can't beat them however you can train yourself to see what they are doing on a price chart and then make money *with* them.

The only way you as a retail investor and trader can make a comfortable income from the market is to educate and train yourself to do so the *right* way. You honestly don't any fancy courses, indicators or a big fancy computer to be successful in this business. I use my 17" HD laptop to work from in the market and that is it. You need to get the right information from the first day in order to the right start.

Learning the right information needed to get started is one of the most critical steps to be a successful market participant over the long term. No one wants to study a lot of information only to find out sometime later that all they needed to know was right there on the chart to begin with.

By the time they realize they have wasted a lot of time and perhaps money on courses and training or books it is very far into their career and business. This only adds to what can be a stressful business as it is anyway. Another thing that happens is that a lot of bad habits can be developed along the way that when brought into a live market situation can be problematic and cause an investor or trader to begin to lose money right away. No one wants that. Let's get you started the right way then right here right now.

Why do you want to be a day trader?

One of the first questions I ask brand new traders who come to me for mentoring is *why* they want to trade. The answer I get *most* of the time is "I want to make money". Hell *we all* want to make money in the market and that should be every investor and traders goal. For me it is to add some money to my account balance monthly as I am a position investor and trader. I look at things on a longer term time horizon.

When I first started out in the business I had not answered any of the serious *"why"* questions and only knew I wanted to make money from trading. I had unrealistic expectations from the start which is only *one* problem most new traders coming into the business have.

Most new people who come into this business have unrealistic expectations on what they will be able to pull out of the market money wise on a daily basis. We have all been there though. Most professionals who are at the level of consistency of making money on a daily basis if they are day traders have accepted that the market will only give out so much and they are good with that.

The live markets are an intimidating and brutal place for someone who starts off with the wrong information. They can be a mysterious, murky, and complicated place for the ill advised. By following the advice in this book and keep it simple and taking very slow and absorbing every detail you can have the best chance for a high probability outcome as a successful market participant. Make no mistake the market can make you lose your mind, burn your soul, and help you to lose all your money. Quickly!!

Learning this business is not sexy however it does not have to be mundane and boring either. It is going to take some time. Most consistently profitable investors and traders I know who have made it have in the very high thousands of hours of screen time.

You can use this book and the references, suggestions and tips in it to go further into your educational studies of the markets and there dynamics. Knowing market dynamics is going to be critical for you to have the winning edge you will need to be a successful market participant. By studying what this book suggests you will not become one of the 97% of the sheeple of the herd.

The live market is not a place for the weak minded or faint hearted. If you have *any* doubts about your skills or confidence take some advice and just stay out of the live market until you have developed a *kill everyone* mentality because that is what you will need to make real money in there every day.

I had the crazy notion in my mind I was going to make $200 a day from trading my first live account. I look back on that now and think how crazy unrealistic that was. Most brand new traders come into the business under funded as it is anyway and I was no different. You cannot go into the live market on a 5 thousand dollar account and expect to make *anything* however your mind is telling that you can.

If you are brand new and have no knowledge in this business, it is critical that you pay attention to the valuable information that is given in this book if you wish to become successful. There are *zero* shortcuts to getting there; however, the learning curve does not have to as brutal as most new people make it on themselves.

Almost all brand new investors and traders from all over the world make the mistakes this book talks about. It's almost universal. Once you have read this entire book, I invite you to tell other people you know who are thinking of getting into this business to also buy it and read it, so *you* can help *them*, as well. Help them save time and money, and they will be grateful to you forever.

The information in this book will put you on the *fast track* to learning exactly the information you need to get started making money right away in the live markets. You want to invest and trade, right? You have to learn it the right way from the start to be able to put what you learn in your education to practical use in the live markets and make consistent profits.

When I say *fast track* I don't mean you can just go in the live market after reading this one book. It is imperative then that since you as a retail investor or trader have a look at all the information you need to study even if you are trading intraday which by the way the smart money does not do.

That should be a huge clue, however because people think this is a get rich quick business when they first get into it and they think that they can learn a few chart patterns and some price action and then can go into the live make and make jet fuel money. New traders are buying Ferrari's and Gulfstream 650's before ever making a live trade with real money.

Don't become one of the sheeple of the herd! Ask yourself this question before you begin your education journey for day trading. Do I want to be the one who *pays* in the market *or* do I want to be the one who *gets* paid? Just keep that in mind when you are learning what you need to know about this business and *it is* a business and you should treat it as such.

You are the one who is in control of what you learn, so I encourage you to do the smart thing and do what it takes to become successful. By reading this entire book, you can reach your desired goals in a shorter time if you just don't do what others are doing wrong. Makes sense, right? Learn from others' mistakes and make yourself better. I encourage you to do it, so you will not lose any of your hard-earned money in the markets.

What are your financial goals from trading?

What kind of investor or trader do you desire to be? You should know this *before* beginning this business. Figure out what style of investing or trading suits your personality the best. Do you want to day trade, swing trade, or position trade? What kind of time are you looking to put in on a daily basis? What kind of returns are you looking at monetarily?

Are you the type of person who has a lot of time to devote to looking at charts in the live market to be a day trader? While I do not recommend day trading, it is possible; however, it requires a lot of time, preparation and a large amount capital. I know very few successful day traders.

Most new people who come into this business have unrealistic expectations on what they will be able to pull out of the market on a daily basis. We have all been there though. Most professionals who are at the level of consistency of making money on a daily basis if they are day traders have accepted that the market will only give out so much and they are good with that.

I had the crazy notion in my mind I was going to make $200 a day from trading my first live account. I look back on that now and think how crazy unrealistic that was. Most brand new traders come into the business under funded as it is anyway and I was no different. You *cannot* go into the live market on a 5 thousand dollar account and expect to make *anything* however your mind is telling that you can.

Setting effective goals is the subject of this chapter and the take away from it should be that all new investors and traders must realize they need to have realistic goals upon coming into the trading business as well as setting attainable goals when they have become established in their trading business.

A new traders goals need to be time and process related, meaning they need to know what they want to accomplish with their trading business from the start and what kind of time frames they would like to have in attaining those goals. Whether you are going to be an investor or an active trader or both, a brand new trader needs to have a strong sense of purpose and desire to succeed at all costs.

I can't stress enough how crucial it is to really think things through before doing anything when entering this business. The outcome of *not* thinking about what you want to get from investing and trading can be a very long and expensive road. It can also be a road paved with gold if done right.

When clients approach me for help I ask them how long they took to research the different types of investing and trading there are and how they came to their decision to become the type of market participant they are currently or aspire to be. Most of the time they haven't thought it through at all and are trying to be all the different types of trader there are I describe here in this book.

I ask them some critical questions as to *why* they want to do this business. I ask them if they know what their long term goals are before they begin their journey into this business. Are they doing it for short term income, or to build up their account? Do they want to build long term wealth? Part of having the right psychology for investing and trading is having all of these questions answered *before* doing anything or studying anything.

I ask them *why* they want to trade. The answer I get most of the time is "I want to make money". *Hell* we *all* want to make money in the market and that should be every investor and traders goal. For me it is to add some money to my account balance monthly as I am a position investor and trader. I look at things on a longer term time horizon.

I try to see if they are trying to get to a profit threshold that will allow them to leave their day job and trade from home? When people can answer these questions properly, it is easy for me to guide them into the right markets, time frames, and build a money making strategy.

I tell all brand new investors and traders I mentor that the *easiest fastest* way for them to reach their goals with trading is to make them practical and achievable to start with. There is no reason to set one's self up for failure from the beginning and sometimes new traders do this to themselves and then wonder why they have failed.

When I first started out in the business I had not answered any of the above questions and only knew I wanted to make money from trading. I had unrealistic expectations from the start which is only one problem most new traders coming into the business have.

The reality of it is that too many undisciplined new traders don't spend enough time composing a rules based plan for the type of trading they wish to do. I have my clients think about what their monetary goals are and then help them compose a great trading plan, becoming a great trader, and attaining their goals.

If you are brand new and have no knowledge in this business, it is critical that you pay attention to the valuable information that is given in this book if you wish to become successful. There are zero shortcuts to getting there; however, the learning curve does not have to as brutal as most new people make it on themselves. Having a realistic outlook is one sure way to speed up your education.

Almost *all* brand new investors and traders from all over the world make the mistakes this book talks about. It's almost universal. Once you have read this entire book, I invite you to tell other people you know who are thinking of getting into this business to also buy it and read it, so *you* can help *them*, as well. Help them save time and money, and they will be grateful to you forever.

The information in this book will put you on the *fast track* to learning exactly the information you need to get started making money right away in the live markets. You want to invest and trade, right? You have to learn it the right way from the start to be able to put what you learn in your education to practical use in the live markets and make consistent profits.

When I say *fast track* I don't mean you can just go in the live market after reading this one book. It is imperative then that since you as a retail investor or trader have a look at all the information you need to study even if you are trading intraday which by the way the smart money does not do.

That should be a huge clue, however because people think this is a get rich quick business when they first get into it and they think that they can learn a few chart patterns and some price action and then can go into the live make and make jet fuel money. New traders are buying Ferrari's and Gulfstream 650's before ever making a live trade with real money.

A great amount of the information put out by the trading industry education wise is not only taught wrong most of the time it is taught unrealistically which also gets brand new traders into trouble from the start. It is most unfortunate for brand new traders coming into the business that they are learning information that can cause them to make a lot of the mistakes detailed in this book and have an unrealistic outlook of the live markets.

They don't know any better because they are new and when they find out how much time and perhaps a lot of their hard earned money they have wasted in the learning things and doing things that have caused them to lose money they are disappointed to put it mildly.

If you are thinking that trading and investing in the live market with your hard earned real money is going to be easy and you are going to make millions of dollars doing it you are in for a rude and very expensive awakening. Don't get me wrong you *can* and *will* make *some* money every day in the live markets perhaps *LOTS OF IT* if you do what it says in this book. I always suggest to new traders that two goals they should have right from the start are to become consistently profitable on a daily basis and to try to add and be able to *keep* some money in their account monthly.

Nothing in the market is guaranteed. It's about putting all the probabilities of having a positive outcome as a market participant in your favor that helps you win. Let's start doing that right now in this book shall we!

The only person who can do it is you

It all starts with *you*. Ultimately it *does* really start with you. It also ends there if you're not diligent in what you do. You are the one who is making the decision to get into the trading and investing business. No one is making you do it. This is a big step for someone to take the plunge into the world of making money with money. One has to look inside one's self and ask some very hard questions before they start driving their own money train down the tracks to riches in the live markets.

The more of these questions you have answered *before* you begin to do anything in this business the better prepared you will be to become successful. There are no guarantees in the market. It is all about preparedness and *you* are the only one making you do this business so I encourage you to listen to the advice given in this section very carefully.

You must have your goals determined *before* you ever even study anything or do anything in this business. To not be prepared is like placing your hand into an open flame. It's very hot and you're going to get burned. Same thing can be said for going into the live financial markets and not having the proper training. Only one thing will happen. *YOU WILL LOSE ALL OF YOUR MONEY!*

Here are some of the things you need to ask yourself and have made a decision on before you get going. Are you trading for short term income? Are you trading to build up an account balance so you can start trading multiple shares? Are you trading for long term wealth goals and/or retirement?

The next thing you need to make a decision on before doing anything is how much money you plan to capitalize your new investing and trading business with. As has been said before and will be said again right here and now. Only trade with money you can afford to lose.

Here is a visualization you can do to get that last sentence in perspective. Picture yourself throwing your starting capital into your barbeque, turning the barbeque all the way up to the highest flame or throwing all your hard earned money into the bon fire at the party you're throwing for yourself for starting your new trading business then watching your money burn up in flames and smoke right before your very eyes.

If you want to swing trade, you will need to have the capital in your account to handle the overnight margin requirement of whatever your chosen instrument is to work in. CAUTION: If you are new and have to use leverage to trade, you just shouldn't trade. Stay out until you have sufficient capital to go into the market and be able to have a chance to make money.

Ask yourself this question. What do you want to be? Are you going to be a stock trader or a futures trader or both? If you are a stock trader have you built a watch list? Do you know how? Do you know how and where to get data about the companies on your watch list? Do you know how to screen for the best stocks? Do you trade large cap, small cap, or micro-cap? What sort of chart do you trade stocks on? Daily, monthly, intraday? Are you a day trader, swing trader or market investor of stocks? You should have all of these questions answered *before* studying anything or ever stepping foot in the live market with real money.

If you would like to be more of an investor or position trader, then you will also need to be well-funded to sustain a draw-down on a position of as much as 50 percent. Should you not have the mental wherewithal to sit through a 50 percent draw-down on any given position in your portfolio, then again I recommend just staying out of the live markets until you have the psychological makeup to do so.

The more you can know in advance before doing anything or studying anything the better you can help yourself to learn only what is needed to get you started in the live market using real money. The rest of what you will need to know can be learned as you go further into the business.

When I first started out, I went to a forum and got help from all the other traders there. It was an atmosphere of camaraderie and sometimes even a little fun competition. It made learning the markets fun. There are traders there from different walks of life with a common goal, and that is to learn to invest and trade in the markets.

I encourage you to find a forum where you fit in and to jump right into the fray and start learning. It is a great way to learn because members share all that they are doing so you can learn not only from your mistakes and triumphs but those of others, as well. It can be a fun way to learn. There are places to learn all types of trading on the Internet now. Find and pick one that best suits the style trading you have chosen to get into.

The one word of caution that I will give here is to be very careful whom you listen to for advice about trading real money. The forums are fun and all; however, there are very few real money traders in these forums. Professional investors and traders don't hang out at those places. The amount that does is less than 1 percent, so *always be careful* to whom you are talking to and listening to in these forums.

The road to success in the business of investing and trading is paved with the wreckage of blown accounts of novice retail traders who did not take the time to do the education, the practice, and the psychological development necessary to become consistently profitable in this business. Don't be *that* trader!

Don't become one of the sheeple of the herd and do what everyone else is doing when and where they are doing it. The smart money can see this on the chart and are looking to take advantage of the errors the sheeple of the herd make over and over again. If you take it slow and try to absorb what is said in this beginners day trading book you can be on your way to giving yourself the financial freedom you're looking from doing this business.

There are no shortcuts to success in investing and trading. You have to do the time if you want to drive the money train. Hopefully if you can get your head around what it says in this book you can be on your way to the bank faster than the other new traders who have not bought this book. This is how you can start to develop your edge over them and make money from them.

The most important thing to do first – education and training

There is a certain progression of things that brand new investors and traders need to know and study. Unfortunately no one tells them in the beginning that most of the information they need is basic and is mostly common sense.

There are absolutely no short cuts. Should any brand new investor and trader decide to try to side step any part of the proper education and training and try to go into the live markets before you have become consistent on a demo account for however long it takes, you stand the chance of your money train going wildly off the tracks and losing all of your risk capital.

No one wants to have that happen however it is the one of the biggest mistakes a brand new investor and trader can make. I have just told you one of the very most important things *not* to do so *don't do it*!

There are a lot of pre-education and pre-trading decisions you will need to make before you spend any money on trading or capitalizing an account to trade live with. This book delivers a set of basic tips to get the proper tools and resources needed to help give you the best information to make some of those hardest decisions.

The most important thing about market education is learning it the right way from the beginning and not making the mistakes that other people are making. Don't become one of the sheeple of the herd. If you learn what *not* to do right from the very start, you will already have an edge over the others who did not take the time to educate themselves this is whom you can actually make money from in the markets once you can see their fear and greed.

You need to do the education and training required and take the proper amount of time developing your rule based plan. You also need to have yourself under control *before* ever stepping foot into the live market with your hard earned real money. To do it any other way is like playing Russian roulette with a completely loaded revolver. You can't win and will get FUBAR!

Remember it takes money to make money and if you go into the live market without the proper training and without a rule based plan with very strict money management you will be out of the game before you are in it.

I strongly encourage you to learn supply and demand trading. Supply and demand is the only thing that makes the markets move. Doesn't it make sense then to only use a method like that to make money for yourself? To me it is no brainer however it took me awhile to *get it* however once I did I turned my trading around and started making money almost overnight.

Look for a supply and demand forum. Go there and learn with the other new traders who are there. You can also do a search online for a foundation and application course for supply and demand. They are online for free for anyone who can find the information. I will have a link to the best thread at the end of the book in the extra links section.

The amount of time it took to become consistently profitable? This amount of time is different for every new investor and trader. For me it was five years from the time I started to study investing and day trading. I love learning so it was not hard for me. I have been fortunate to have already had a high degree of education. It takes a long time to take in and digest all the information needed to go through all the steps of becoming a professional investor and trader especially an intraday trader.

Time is on the new investors and trader's side however they do not recognize this because all they see are dollar signs. They want take short cuts and try to move to fast so they can start making quick money in the markets. They don't know that the market is always going to be there waiting to pay them. There is a line in a Glen Frye song smuggler's blues that says "the lure of easy money has a very strong appeal". That may well be true however if you have not done the proper education and training the right way for this business you will be cruising down the boulevard of broken dreams watching the smoking wreckage of your burned out account in the rearview mirror.

They say hindsight is 20/20 in investing and trading. I say if you can just take the time to train your eyes to see what you need to see to make money wouldn't you want to do that? It took me a good long while to realize this however once I did and accepted the good and the bad of what happens in this business I was there. I spend maybe 30 minutes a week looking at charts now. That's it.

There is no reason to be in a rush in the market. Time is on your side if you have learned how to use it to your advantage. It is really about price and time in the live market. Once you have learned to see where the price of the instruments you are working in regularly make their moves from, and where they are going to go to with a high degree of certainty, you have a distinct advantage over the sheeple of the herd who try to do the opposite of what the market is actually doing and make mistakes. Learn to see them making their mistakes and you can profit from them.

In trading live with real money it is all about stacking the odds of having a positive outcome in your favor. Professionals are only looking for a low risk high reward high probability positive outcome. They know what they are doing before they do it. How long does it take to get to this level of understanding and proficiency? As long as it takes! There is no rule book that says you have to be in the market at a certain time. The market is always going to be there!

Being an investor and trader is the best business in the world I think. I know of no other business in the world where someone is actually handing you money. In the live market you can get paid handsomely everyday provided you know what you are doing. For the sheeple of herd who study the same thing, do the same things when everyone else seems to be doing it where they are doing it from they have no chance really. They have been programmed to do it wrong from the start and continue to do it wrong until they blow up their account and have to quit. Don't become one of the sheeple of the herd! Sounds kind of like the title to an old B horror movie or a cult.

Professionals are getting paid from the sheeple of the herd because they can see the mistakes the sheeple of the herd are making on a continuous basis. All the professionals are doing is just watching and waiting for the same mistakes to be made over and over to get paid. It is pretty much a transfer of accounts of those who have not done the right education from the start to those who have. Ask yourself this question. Do you want to be the one who is paying OR do you want to be the one who *gets* paid?

The first things you need to know – how to read a price chart and price action

There is really no easy way to do it honestly. There is a certain progression of steps *all* new traders must go through to be able to drive their own money train to the bank on a daily basis which I have detailed in the book.

This book will start the new equities trader the right way to begin driving their money train down the right tracks directly to the bank. By knowing what to study from the start you can *greatly reduce* the huge learning curve there is in this business to be able to make money in the live markets on a consistent daily basis.

There is a certain progression of steps that every new equities trader (or any trader) must follow to become a consistently profitable professional trader. There are absolutely no short cuts. Should any brand new trader decide to try to side step any part of the proper education and training and try to go into the live markets before you have become consistent on a demo account for however long it takes, you stand the chance of your money train going wildly off the tracks and possibly losing *all* of your capital.

I wrote this book for people who want to become investors and traders in today's financial markets, but have zero experience and are looking for the best quality information to get them started. If you pay attention to the information in this book you can avoid becoming one of the 'sheeple of the herd.' Don't get yourself fleeced up beyond account recovery (FUBAR)!

While this book is mainly focused on the stock investor and trader, the core of what is presented in this book is how *ALL* markets work which is on the principle of supply and demand. There is no mention of anything other than what needs to be learned from the start of your investing and trading career. It is learning supply and demand investing and trading and price action. That's what you need to focus on from the start if you want to be successful right away.

This book will be an incredible read as an introduction for someone has zero or very little experience in the equities market can expect to research and learn if they want to have any chance at being successful making real money in the live markets. If you're brand new this book will give you a start, if you have a little knowledge already I hope this book can give you more and help you learn something new.

I have tried to write this book in plain enough language so that the information can be understood by anyone even if English is not the native language. This book is short and to the point and gives the first advice needed for brand new traders interested in the stock market.

I purposely do not put any charts in this book so that you can read and absorb what is said without being distracted by a bunch of fancy colorful candle charts. You'll have plenty of time for that. Trust me! Laughing out loud here.

Instead of trying to read this book fast I recommend that you go slow and look up and search for the main things the book talks about that will help you to become successful right away. Skip over anything that is important and it could for sure cause you to lose some money. No one wants that now right?

If you need to study each thing one at a time so you can fully grasp it, so be it. You do not need to be in any hurry. The market is always going to be there waiting to give you a chance to make money.

The progression of steps is to learn money management, gain a hold on your own psychology, learn to read the price charts of the instruments you choose to work in and finally learn how to quantify real supply and demand in the live market to make your trade decisions from.

You will also need to make a rule based plan which should be based on the type of trading you wish to do as well as what time frame you wish to do it on. You should learn to journal your market activity both on demo and in the live market. There are plenty of journal templates on line that you can download and use as a baseline for your own, and then once you are prepared the right way you can add or delete information from your journal as needed.

There are a lot of pre-education and pre-trading decisions you will need to make before you spend any money on trading or capitalizing an account to trade live with. This book delivers a set of *basic* tips to get the proper tools and resources needed to help give you the best information to make some of those hardest decisions.

What this book is *not* going to do is give you a system. You will need to learn to develop that on your own because every investor and trader is different. What works for one investor or trader *will not* work for another. You will develop your own method or system based on the type of investing and trading you wish to do.

Many brand new investors and traders think they need to learn it all when first starting out, and that couldn't be further from the truth. They get into overload or "analysis paralysis." It doesn't have to be that hard, and it's not. If you continue reading this book, you will save yourself a lot of time and gain a steeper learning curve.

To optimize your education time, as I said you need to have *already* determined what you want to accomplish. There is no point in wasting the valuable time of your mentor, including your own, if you do not have an idea of what you want out of the markets. It is best to just stay out until you know what you want to accomplish.

A friend of mine who introduced me to the business said something to me once that hit me like he had punched me in the face. He said, "Why would you want to learn a bunch of different things instead of knowing a few things that consistently make you money every day?"

My advice to the new equities traders is to learn the price action of one to three stocks intimately to start, and then once they are familiar with them and become consistently profitable working in those stocks, they begin adding more shares to those positions.

Remember you don't need to know everything all at once, merely what makes *you* money. If you can remember this last statement, you are on your way to success in the business of equities trading. When you are done reading this book you will have an excellent basic explanation of *what* and *what not* to do before you even study anything or do any kind of education. The information will put you on the *fast track* to becoming a successful self-directed equities trader with very little money invested other than the cost of this first book.

How long does this education and learning take? There is no timetable set in stone. As someone new to this business it is critical you have all the information you need, and that you fully understand it and are able to act on it in the real-time live markets with real money. Going into the live markets and using your real money to invest and trade without educating yourself is like playing Russian roulette with a completely loaded revolver. Why would you do that to yourself?

The first basic knowledge that a new investor and trader needs to learn is to how to read a price chart, read price action of the instruments they desire to work within, learn how to use supply and demand value areas to trade from. Mastering these skills and becoming competent at them is critical to being able to move forward and becoming consistently profitable.

Price only moves up sideways or down. It can't be that hard to learn right? It is all other information coming at an investor and trader which cause them to fumble and make mistakes. New investors and traders make mistakes because they do not take the proper time to learn how to read a price chart and the price action of the asset they want to work in.

Learning to read a price chart properly takes some time and learning to read the price action of a specific instrument can take a long time to get to know all the nuances of the price action of that particular market. It does not happen overnight. All the information an investor or trader needs is right there on the chart in front of them they just have to train their eyes to see it.

Along with chart reading goes with looking to only enter at low risk high reward high probability value areas. These supply and demand value areas are where price action makes its turns in the live markets. Price turns there because that is where the unfilled orders of the smart money reside at in the live market. Price is clearly out of balance at this area.

Once you have trained your eyes to see where these value areas are on a price chart you will have an edge that the 97% of the sheeple of the herd do not have and you can start making money from the mistakes they make. These supply and demand value areas are easy to spot once you know *what* you are looking for and *where* to look for it on the chart.

The retail sheeple of the herd make their mistakes over and over and over again at these value areas. Learn to see the sheeple of the herd making their mistakes and profit from them over and over and over. It is beautiful! Here is a tip: The retail sheeple of the herd make these two mistakes over and over again. The *first* one is that they enter the market *after* a huge move up or down. The *second* is that they enter where price is *known* to be out of balance and supply exceeds demand or demand exceeds supply.

The smart money also leaves huge tracks in the market when they move price with their power and money. They can't hide this footprint they leave and it is your job to track them and then do what they are doing where they are doing it from. They take price to the areas where they want to get more orders filled at a certain price. See them on the chart and ride on their backs and make money along with them.

That is how I make money in the live markets every day. I just look for where the smart money have their resting orders and then wait for the retail sheeple of the herd to make their mistakes and buy or sell to or from them and then follow the smart money to where they are going to next. You don't need an MBA degree from a big fancy college for that! Combine price action with supply and demand investing and trading and you have an edge over the retail sheeple of the herd.

Knowing money management can save you money

Being wrong in trading isn't *wrong* however *staying wrong* in trading will be death to your account! Your job in your investing and trading business is to be a money manager not a money maker. You get paid to take risks yes, however you have to an expert at controlling them. The money is just a byproduct of that function.

All of the people I know in this business who are money makers actually do not even worry about making money. There sole focus is preserving the capital they already have. They manage their risk on every position at all costs and know that they can have a loser every now and then and are ok with it.

All consistently profitable investors and traders I personally know have a risk plan or strategy. By following this plan they have no worries about losing money and accept that it could happen. They have found what works for them in the live markets and just follow the plan to make their money every day. If a set up they are looking at does not meet their plan criteria they just do not take action.

The main reason why they are so successful is because they stick to their plan no matter if they are losing money or making a lot of money. They do not deviate from their plan because they know that over a long period of time they will be consistently profitable from having done so.

These people have developed an edge over the sheeple of the herd and exploit them with their edge to make money from them every day. They know what mistakes the sheeple of the herd make over and over again on a daily basis and so does the smart money.

The successful investor or trader then just watches for the smart money to make their move on the sheeple of the herd and then just capitalize right along with them on their power and volume. They know that the herd does not trade with a plan and can see their errors because of it.

The consistently profitable investor and trader only enters a position based on their plan which normally calls for the stop loss and profit target to be already known before the position is even entered. I personally use an automated entry so there is no emotion in it. I just set the entry parameter in the live market and when I am filled everything is done for me. All I need do at that point is wait to get paid. There is zero stress, zero drama, and zero complications.

There is no letting a position that is in profit come back to turn into a loser due to having the stop loss already in the live market. I have entered the position *already knowing* what my stop loss amount is money wise so there is no question as to how much I will lose should the position not work out as planned. Once the profit target is hit the position automatically closes and then it is time to look for the next opportunity.

Profitable investors and traders know they can make consistent profits over time and do not look to make all their money on one or two big positions. They realize and accept they will have a higher probability of having a positive outcome over many successful outcomes in the market versus just a few. They only are looking for the lowest risk highest reward positions and will just wait until the opportunity arises. When the opportunity *does* come they are decisive and take immediate action. Once the action has completed they look for the next one.

I always suggest learning risk management and money management first when mentoring new investors and traders coming into the business that come to me for help. It is the one thing that in the course of my own education and training spent a little time on however not enough. It is one the thing that can save you from having a catastrophic financial outcome in the business.

Once you have studied risk management and then apply it to how you want to invest and trade you can begin to have some success as long as you stick to your money management plan and never deviate from it.

This is where most retail traders get themselves into trouble and cause themselves to lose money. They will set a stop loss and then when price action approaches the stop they will adjust it or take it out altogether.

Risk in investing and trading is unavoidable however with the proper training and a good sound risk plan can be diminished when the plan is followed. Risk is also diminished over time when the investor and trader gains more knowledge as to how much appetite for risk they really have. Without this knowledge the investor or trade cannot gain an understanding or get the experience and competence to make consistent profits.

Taking on larger risk and trading more size does not necessarily mean bigger profits it just means bigger risk is taken to get the profits. Size is earned not a given and this is where the 97% of people who fail at this business make a major error. They think they can trade size on a retail account and beat the market. They might do it once or twice however I tell clients they must be considering the long term to be truly consistently profitable.

To be consistently profitable over the long term one must consider capital preservation their number one rule. To be successful in this business it cannot be any other way. It takes money to make money in the market and _once your money is gone it is gone_. This is why I tell clients they must study risk and money management first and foremost.

All professional investors and traders I know will say the same thing if asked what is the number one thing they consider to be important in their business. That is capital preservation. If you lose all your money in the market you can't *be* in the market.

Even if you were careless and lost only 50% of your capital you would still need to make 100% to get all your money back. It is possible to do this albeit very hard and not likely, especially for the retail sheeple of the herd. Once they begin to lose money they will start to jump around to different asset classes and systems. This only compounds their problems.

I ask my clients are you in the business to make money or lose it? Do you want to spend your time making your money back or making real profits? The answer should be a given however most of the time they come to me after it is too late and they have done themselves catastrophic damage in their accounts.

Capital preservation should be seen as the long term goal and not based on short term needs. It is very important to have figured out what your money goals are *before* you step foot into the markets with your hard earned real money. Questions I ask are: are you trading for short term income or long term wealth building? Are you trying to build up your account balance to be able to take on more risk and trade larger size?

If a client cannot answer these questions right away I just encourage them to stay out of the live markets until they can answer them and be honest. I also will ask them how much capital they plan to enter the live markets to work with. There is no point in trying to enter the live markets with scared money.

The capital one starts their business with should be capital that is disposable. Meaning that if all the capital happened to be lost to the markets the investor or trader would not be hurt by the loss in any way. I have clients I mentor do that visualization I was talking about earlier in this book. I have them think about throwing their starting capital into their barbeque and turning it on and watching their money burning up in flames and smoke.

It sounds harsh I know, however the reality of it is that when a new investor or trader who has entered the business is not using a rules based plan, has not done the proper education and training and learned what they need to know to take only high probability positions that will give the highest reward and have the lowest risk the outcome is virtually almost always the same. Flames and smoke!

The road to success for investors and traders does not have to be paved with the smoking wreckage of their burned out account. It can be a road paved with gold provided they have taken all the right measures to ensure they will have the best possible outcome of being a successful market participant.

The best principle in risk management can be stated in three words. "Use a stop"! No one, especially a brand new trader or investor can be prepared enough for the volatility and brutality of the live market. It is fine to practice on a demo account to learn your software platform for entries and exits however it is completely another thing to be able to do it in a live market environment with the best market participants in the world who are trying to take your money. Keep it simple, be prepared, have a plan and watch your money and you can't go wrong.

Your ego won't be needed here

Check your ego at the door please it doesn't belong in here. The first things I will say here is that in live market trading you need to check your ego at the door. In the live market your ego *is not* your amigo! There is a line in a song that comes to mind here. "Check yourself before you wreck yourself".

Too many times I see brand new traders coming in thinking they can outsmart the market. Guess what you can't. You are the one who is going to get FUBAR. This part of this book will serve as a guide for the brand new investor and trader with zero experience and give you a starting point as to what to study and where to go to get more information on trading psychology. There are plenty of articles out there on trading psychology and I encourage you to read the ones that may pertain to any issues you may think you have before beginning in this business.

You must be true to yourself from the start in this business. Only when an investor or trader has experienced hard losses or even blown out their account do they start to work on their psychology for investing and trading. They have ignored the subject from the start of their education and training and not bothered to look inside themselves.

Unfortunately they wait too long and try to un-do the bad habits which have already been developed. This is very hard to do and sometimes too little too late. This is why I put this psychology part second in the first things a brand new trader needs to know. It is a very important aspect of the learning process which needs to take place before going in the live markets with real money.

If you are brand new to investing and trading that's great. You can learn the reality of how investing and trading works in the real market from the very beginning of your career in this business by reading this entire book. If you are already in the business and struggling with your investing and trading and losing money, I would encourage you to step back and study supply and demand investing and trading. You'll be glad you did and so will your account!

One thing about learning trading is it is going to take a while. I have a very high degree of education and thought to myself "how long could it freakin take"? It took me a total of 5 years. All the traders I blogged with and learned with at the forum I was learning at all told me the same thing. You just have to go slow.

Don't be the trader who *pays* be the trader who *gets* paid. Learn to do this business the right way from the beginning and you won't be the one who is the *payer* you will be the *payee*. If you learn this business right and can become successful you will have the skills which will last you the rest of your life that will enable you to make money from anywhere you are in the world that has WI-FI. You will have the skills which will last you the rest of your natural life until the day you CASH OUT.

No one can know what the market is going to do at any given time. What you *can* and *should* already know though is what you are going to do if the market starts to go against you. This is what you are in control of. You must have the discipline to follow whatever rules you have in your plan that tell you what you will do when this happens and do it with complete calm.

By now if you have read this far, this book might be scaring the crap out of you. That is probably a good thing. If you are brand new and want to really *do* this business and are not just playing around you should plan to *not* do these mistakes and take as long as you need to take with your learning curve. The market is *always* going to be there waiting to pay you!

One thing I can tell you that is an absolute about the live market is that there are people in there who will walk over dead bodies to get paid and make money. They will carve your account up like it is a Thanksgiving turkey and not break a sweat. It's nothing personal. They don't know you, care about you or care if you lose all your money to them. It's just business as usual every day.

The reality of the market is that there are people in there who are smarter than you, have waaaaaaaay more money than you, have better algo than you and are trying to take your money and transfer it from your account to theirs. Are you going to *let* that happen?

Here are some things to ask yourself before you begin your investing and trading education and training. Am I the type of individual who is impulsive, tend to worry a lot? Can I remain calm in very tense circumstances? Can I be decisive when it comes time to make a hard decision? Do I have the ability to follow rules and follow a plan of action? Can I solve complex problems while under pressure?

If you can answer these questions honestly to yourself you may have a good chance at becoming a successful investor and trader. If you are not able to be truthful with yourself I will be brutally honest with you here, perhaps it might be best to look at another profession.

You must build a rock solid foundation of principles to work from in investing and trading and a psychological base is no different than the trading base. You must have it from the beginning to become successful. You must develop structure and discipline that is unbending.

Having structure and discipline are traits of the most successful investors and traders. Having these two traits among others are critical to being a professional self-directed investor and trader. Without them it will be very hard to become consistently profitable on a daily basis.

The most successful investors and traders I associate with have all mastered themselves and their own psychology. They know what makes them tick (no pun intended). They have overcome the need to simply make money and have become focused on the preservation of capital and know that making money is a byproduct of that.

When clients come to me for mentoring one of the first things I ask them is if they have looked inside themselves. The only place a trader becomes successful from is within. A mentor or a trading coach can only help a new investor or trader so much. New aspiring investors and traders must look within themselves and figure out what they need to do to enhance and perfect their performance in the live market.

I tell all new investors and traders they must have their emotions under control *before* they ever set foot in the live markets and put their hard earned money to work. It is one thing to learn how to execute your trading plan on a demo account to learn how the platform you will be utilizing to place your positions in the live market. It is entirely another thing to do it in a live market environment with the best market participants in the world.

Once you have your psychology and emotions under control you will achieve consistency and be able to make as much money in the live markets as you desire. Combine that with solid money management principles and you will have become a professional investor and trader.

You can do a simple search for "trading psychology" online and do more research as to what you need to know and how you can overcome any issues you may have *before* making any costly mistakes. This is what it takes to become a professional in this business.

<<<>>><<<>>>

Learn a method that works in any market

Through nobody's fault but their own, retail 'sheeple of the herd' get into trouble from day one by not pursuing the right education. They do themselves a disservice by not taking the proper amount of time needed to become proficient in the supply and demand method of trading.

They try to rush into the market before becoming consistently profitable on a daily basis on demo, which is a critical step in developing your edge and also getting to know the platform from which you will be trading in the live markets. Demo trading is the best way to gain experience *BEFORE* going into the live markets with real money.

Why they continue to do this is beyond me as there many stories in circulation about people who have done this and lost all of their money. When will they listen and learn? Seems like it is always after it is too late and they are already out of the game.

It's real simple. Another problem retail investors and traders make for themselves is that they over complicate strategies when it all needs to be simple. The principle of supply and demand is a very simple market principle that has been around since there were markets. The training is not that hard to do for this style of investing and trading, yet people tend to want to not listen and go against the grain.

Remember what I said about the smart money being willing to walk over dead bodies to make money? They are there to take your money every day. It's nothing personal. They are the herders of the 'sheeple of the herd.' It is one thing to learn what to do in supply and demand investing and trading. However, it is another animal entirely to be able to execute your plan in the live market with real money.

Use price action with supply and demand to have a lethal double whammy edge over the sheeple of the herd who have all studied the wrong information from the start on day one and have been taught unrealistic information that will not help them in any way in the live market. Use price action with supply and demand with sound money management and a detailed trading plan for whatever instruments you desire to work in and there should be no reason you cannot make *some* money every day in the live market once you have studied and prepared yourself properly.

No one can predict what will happen in the live markets. There are too many things going on all at one time. You can however see with a high degree of certainty where the markets will go to if you know what to look for and where to look for it. If you use supply and demand as your guide in your trading and investing you will know exactly what to do.

You want to have a winning edge from the very beginning? Go out on the internet and find a supply and demand foundation and application course. I encourage you to watch every video and read every article and book you can on this style of investing and trading. I highly encourage you to study this supply and demand method at length as it will greatly cut down your learning curve and enable you to begin to make real money in the live markets from the very start of your trading and investing business once you get it up and running.

You do not need to over think *ANYTHING* in supply and demand (S&D) trading. It is very simple, the simplest in fact. I had to unlearn 95% of what I had already studied before I became consistently profitable on a daily basis in the markets. My goal is to save you brand new traders and investors who are new and wanting to learn financial market trading a lot of time and cut down your learning curve so you can be on your way to making real money in the live markets every day. How fast you "get it" is up to you.

Here is a good start for you brand new investors and traders looking to understand supply and demand dynamics and use it to invest and trade in the live markets of today. It is economics 101 pretty much. You should learn it though if you want to know and understand what really makes price do what it does in the live market because it is this and nothing else.

So that I do not sound redundant in my explanations after we move on from this point I will direct you to go here: http://www.investopedia.com/university/economics/economics 3.asp for an explanation of the dynamics of supply and demand which will from this point be the only thing mentioned as far as a way of investing and trading is concerned in the live markets.

Supply and demand is not rocket science and no one owns it, or has a patent on it and anyone can learn it. It is a simple market principle that has been in existence since there was a market. It will always be the same principle till there is no more market which will be the end of days.

You do not have to be a math wizard to get it and you do not have to memorize any formulas or math equations. It is just a simple yet powerful principle that when armed with its knowledge and the knowledge of the price action of your chosen instruments of choice you can have a serious winning edge which will give you the highest probability of having a positive outcome on being a market participant.

It all builds off of this basic core principle of supply and demand right here so I encourage you to take you time and absorb it a little at a time. You will see that it is a robust and repeatable process in any liquid market and any time frame. It does not matter if you are trading equities, spot or forex futures, grains or kittens and puppies for that matter. You just have to pick what TF (time frame) you like and what market(s) you want to invest in or trade and what your comfort level of risk is in those markets. As I said it is fairly simple once you have it down pat.

Back in the day the traders in the pit and at the banks didn't have computers and barely had charts. It was time, price and unfilled orders that they had to tell them information. Stacks of papers on the desk. If you see older news footage or movie scenes and the floor of the exchange and pits are littered with papers what do think those papers were? They were filled orders. Filled orders are what you see to the left of current PA. Doesn't mean *ANYTHING* they are filled. What you are able to tell from this data though is where the unfilled orders are by seeing where PA left from abruptly. What does that look like on a price chart? You need to know this to be able to see where PA will go to and also come back to get more unfilled orders.

Everything you see on the chart to the left has already taken place hence why all indicators except price action are lagging and of no use to a professional Forex trader. The *ONLY* thing that matters is where those unfilled orders are resting in the market because *THAT* is where PA goes to and takes off from. The only *other* thing that matters is how much time price spent there at that price level. Learn how to read PA in this manner and you will have a high probability of making money every single day. Combine that with supply and demand dynamics and it will be all you ever have to know to make money in the live markets the rest of your natural life. *PROVIDED YOU HAVE MONEY LEFT!!!*

Supply and demand investing and trading works on all asset classes on any time frame. All you need to do is train your eyes to see where the value areas that the smart money are buying and selling from and then do what they do where they are doing it. It is of no concern to you *why* they are doing it only *WHEN* and

WHERE they are doing it. It really does not get any easier than this truthfully.

Supply and demand value areas on a price chart represent *ALL* buyers and sellers in the world who are in the live market you are looking at that time and thus it is very easy to quantify were the unfilled orders reside in the live market. As I have stated all you need to do is train your eyes to spot these value areas on the price chart you are analyzing and then make a decision whether you would like to become a market participant as well.

Mostly all of the professional traders I associate with have in the very high thousands of hours of screen time to get good at seeing and opening positions from supply and demand value areas on charts. Hopefully you will get good at it as well and become well off by doing so. The amount of screen time needed to be able to go in the live market and make real money is said to be 10,000 or more hours. Hopefully this book will help get you started and cut down that amount of learning curve time.

It is your job to practice to get good at recognizing the value areas. You will need to do it over and over and over again until it becomes second nature for you to spot, quantify and execute a position from these value areas without hesitation. As soon as you have learned and have the experience you can open positions from them in the live real markets with real money with confidence and zero fear.

What you are looking for is the way PA leaves the certain area which is said to be a supply or demand value area. This value area is also sometimes called a base or PA can be said to be basing. This is that sideways price action I was talking about earlier.

It is critical that you train your eyes to recognize these areas to acquire your positions from. This is where price is in balance for the moment. The way PA leaves this value area is a key piece of data for you to use in your analysis of any position you may be thinking of taking in the live market with real money. PA will normally leave a value area when it is out of balance with a huge move in PA.

This huge move is normally seen as a large expanded range candle (ERC) or a bunch of them. Does not matter what color you make your candles and I suggest you just have them the same color as the color of the candles will make no difference as to what data the candle is telling you. All that matters is that you understand and become an expert at what to see, quantify it and where it is happening. When PA comes back and revisits this value area again in the future is when you want to be there waiting with your resting order in the live market.

Remember this: first come first served. Which means if your order is already there resting in the live market in the queue you have a high probability of being filled right away verses adding your order and having to wait in line with all the other orders just going in.

The way PA leaves the supply and demand value areas is also the way in tends to return to it. Meaning PA can blast back into the area with a nice big ERC or if it left the value area slowly it can meander its way back. Another way PA can leave a value area is by gapping up or down. What PA is coming back to this value area for is to fill more of the unfilled orders which were left there when price became out of balance the first time it was at this area.

What matters most is that we see where the smart money is deploying their assets and what best pricing they are looking for. We want to get it at what price they get it for. Believe your eyes and not your brains. It's the smart money's ginormous footprints that they leave all over our charts that really matter. It is their tracks in the market that you are looking for on your price chart in the price action of your chosen instrument. They are easy to spot once you know what you are looking for.

Once you are armed with this knowledge it does not matter what you are investing in or trading. These signals I am telling you to see are the only thing that moves price action on a chart. Any chart. Even kittens and puppies if you trade them! If you keep it simple from the start of your learning and education those skills will follow you into the live markets and be beneficial to you in making real money every day.

That's the beauty of it this method. It works on all liquid markets and on any time frame you choose to look at it on. I encourage you to work on daily charts because that is what the smart money uses. Once you can see the value areas on the daily chart you can see them on any time frame. That's what makes this method so lethal. It's the combination of price action and supply and demand value areas. That is what wins in today's markets.

Learn to see unfilled orders on a price chart and the PA of your preferred instrument to trade and you are home. No fancy news, no indicators just PA and what makes the market do what it does, supply and demand. It's *THE* only thing that makes the market move.

Simple really, however traders tend to make things hard on themselves and cause a lot account pain because of it. Don't be that investor or trader. People just think this is a get rich quick business. It's precisely the opposite unless you are a bank or hedge fund and you are using leverage and OPM (other people's money) or a combination of both.

In S&D it's all about setting your position order and then just *waiting* and letting PA come to you. It's just a waiting game at that point. If you get filled there then you are in the market with everything already there. *IF* you do not get filled then you just cancel the order and reassess PA and look for the next signal and opportunity.

The thing about supply and demand style trading is that you either have to be there when PA reaches where you need it to be *OR* have a resting limit order in the market for when it does.

That is going to take some getting used to. The whole position order needs to go in at the same time on a trade like that. Stop loss and profit target need to go in with the trade especially the stop loss.

If you know how to build out the chart properly you should in fact have an idea where and when PA will get to where you need it be to capitalize on it. You can make big money with the smart money not withstanding HFT's, Algo or AMM. You can't fight that in any way nor should you even try to. Hopefully you are on the right side of it and PA can sail right to your PT on the smart money's volume.

If you are still having trouble seeing the value areas I encourage you to go back and analyze why? Ask yourself these questions. Have you looked back far enough left? Are you using multiple time frames (MTF) to do analysis? Does it help you to understand how to look for and evaluate PA on higher time frame (HTF) charts and how get the curve as well? Look in your journal and analyze what you have done previously that worked and did not. Then just do what *did* work for you over and over and over again!

There are a lot of other ways and extra things like probability boosters to aid the trader in the use of supply and demand that are beyond the scope of this basic book. I will have another book coming up soon that details how to use probability boosters to see more trade set ups so be looking for that book soon at all of your favorite booksellers online.

Only work from a rule based plan

In live market trading it helps to keep the decision making process as consistent and objective as possible. Using a rules based plan for your trading is a *must* and is a trait all successful investors and traders I know possess. A winning plan should be able to sustain your profitability over time in order that you can *keep* all your hard earned profits you make from the markets.

The reality of it is that too many undisciplined new traders don't spend enough time composing a rules based plan for the type of trading they wish to do. I have my clients think about what their monetary goals are and then help them compose a great trading plan, becoming a great trader, and attaining their goals.

There is no room for excuses in the professional traders mind and thus they know that they are the final decision maker on what is being done or *NOT* done. They are in complete control of all aspects of their trading plan. They have mastered keeping their emotions fully controlled and are aware they are in control of the destiny of there long term investment strategy and management of their portfolio. This is one of the things that make them so successful and it is *all done by following their rule based plan.*

I tell *all* new people I help out that what you will find is that over the course of your learning curve and time in the live markets that you will ultimately find that what is going to work for you and make you money every day or month is a combination of things you have learned over time and have put together to make *your own* winning rule based plan. What works for one trader *will not* work the same way for another however that does not mean you cannot adapt different ideas to fit your own trading style.

Developing a trading plan takes a lot of hard work sometimes as much if not more than actually learning how to trade and operate your platform. It takes time to see what works for you and what does not. It also takes a lot of time to develop the rules that go along with your trading plan. Having a plan and some rules are critical in this business. To not have them and stick to them is a recipe for financial disaster and account ruin.

All traders who have become consistently profitable use a solid uncomplicated rule based plan. They have achieved their long term success by properly executing their plan flawlessly over and over and over again. They are prepared at all times and this is just one of the traits that make them successful.

It doesn't matter how many or how few rules you have in your plan. Most investors and traders I know who are consistently profitable on a daily basis have a simple plan that is perhaps one page or less. It is one thing to have a plan it is however the most important thing to do is to *follow the plan at all costs*. I always say if you are a known rule breaker then just don't too many however you must have *some*.

One exercise I like my clients to do to get them in the habit of following their plan is to pretend they are an airline pilot and they have to follow a checklist at all times and never break any procedural rules or all lives could be lost. Airline pilots by the way are some of the best investors and traders out there in the business today. They are used to doing what I just described and will not deviate for any reason.

Take the last paragraph and just imagine that your account balance is the lives and if you do not follow your plan *all* of your money could be lost. Make no mistake you can perhaps lose *all* of your money by not having and following a plan.

Successful investors and traders know that that having a simple plan is the only way to have a profitable significant edge in the live markets. A plan does not have to be complicated to be successful and these consistently profitable investors and traders have come to realize this and actually use the simplest methods in investing and trading which is supply and demand.

One of the things that traders do is they get monitoring their positions confused with trade management. If you have followed your rules based plan and determined your entry and exit as well as your stop loss and profit target there should be nothing to do really.

What I mean by monitoring your position is to make sure your automated strategy if you are using one is doing what it is supposed to be doing. This is critical as even the best automated strategy can have a discombobulation at some point.

A well-known Forex educator said in one of his webinars I listened to some time ago that he is a big advocate of always monitoring positions. He had been using an automated robot to assist in putting on positions. His robot started to put on positions and malfunctioned. What happened to him was he lost 30% of his live account working capital in 24 hours because he was not monitoring what was happening.

I only recommend using an automated system if you are using it for putting on and taking off positions as well as executing a stop loss and profit target at the same time as the position is being executed in the live market. Then it is truly hands off. All you need to do at that point is to **keep your hands off** the mouse and let the market do all the heavy lifting for you. *Can* you do that?

Until you can monitor your live market positions without actually doing *anything* I strongly recommend that you stay out of the real live market with your hard earned real money. Just because you are monitoring what is going on *does not* mean you have to take any action!

The sooner you can get your head around that last statement the more money you will be able to make. That's is what you are in this business for so have some control and do what needs to be done to become successful. Be disciplined and don't make the mistakes this book details. Do not become one of the sheeple of the herd and do what everyone else does and study what everyone else studies.

Learn to think independently and make money for yourself for the rest of your life!

If you think like smart money you'll make money like them

After having read this entire book you will hopefully know how to have the self-control and patience to wait until price gets to where *you* need it to be to enter the market with confidence. Patience means points! It can take a while to develop this part of the mindset and mentality needed to be a consistently profitable investor and trader. I know it did for me. Once I had my 'AHH ha!' moment, there was no looking back.

Banks and institutions are in the business to make money plain and simple. All they care about are two things and that is time and price which I have talked a bit about already in the book. The only thing they are in business for is to make a profit. Who are they making the all the loot from though? It's the retail trader that's who. They can see they retail sheeple of the herd making their mistakes on a price chart and just take advantage of them over and over and over again on a daily basis.

It's no secret that Wall Street banks make huge profits. It is in your face in the media on a daily basis. How do they actually make this huge profit though? They make their huge profits by controlling their risk on the positions they take. All they care about is protecting their risk capital when it is exposed in the live markets. We are talking about in the billions of dollars perhaps even a trillion dollars at any given moment.

All traders who have become consistently profitable including all the Wall Street banks and institutions use a solid uncomplicated rule based plan. They have achieved their long term success by properly executing their plan flawlessly over and over and over again. They are prepared at all times and this is just one of the traits that make them successful. Make no mistake about it you had better be *completely prepared* to work in the live market before you ever set foot in there with the smart money.

Every professional investor and trader I associate with treats investing and trading as a business and so should you. Having a plan to do your business is the most important aspect of making money in the investing and trading business especially when your real money is on the line in the live market. If you wish to be a consistently profitable investor and trader in today's live market and survive, build your plan to do so. Build your plan around what your intended goals are, the Wall Street banks do.

Trading to win every day is what these professional people and the Wall Street banks do. You are looking at the same information on your charts as every other trader in the world looking at that chart you are on. The question is do *you* see it how *they* see it? You need to see what the banks and institutions see and you also need to be able to spot the sheeple of the herd retail traders making their mistakes also. You can profit from both groups if you know how and are prepared properly to do so.

When you have learned how to read the price action of the instruments you have chosen to work in to make you money in the live market you should have no problems making money with the smart money. The markets are there for everyone to make money every day all you have to do is go in there and get it. I always say "see what they see do what they do".

The only problem with that is that *everyone else* is trying to do that also. It all goes back to preparedness to work in the live market. If you should decide to go in there and are unprepared or even underprepared you will assuredly lose some money right away and perhaps even *all* of it. Don't be *that* trader!

I always love saying, "I don't care *why* they're doing it, I only care *when* and *where* they are doing it from!" This is what you need to educate yourself to do. Educate yourself properly. All the rest is BS and won't help you at all in the live market.

If I have said it once I have said it one hundred million times. No one wants to lose $200-$300 on a 50-50 set up however if you have 4-5 trading days or months or years the $300 becomes immaterial because you were prepared for the best possible high probability outcome. The only trades you should be in are the ones that offer you a high probability of gaining a profit. How are you going to afford fuel for your money train or your G650 if you are taking low risk low reward trades?

The absolute only way you as a retail sheeple of the herd trader or investor will be able to make a living in the live market on a consistent daily basis is to be 100% confident in your skills and have zero fear or apprehension about being decisive when it comes time to pull the trigger on a live trade.

To make a living as a professional trader and doing it intraday you will need to be trading a very large risk capital account. I *strongly advise* against day trading unless you have a very large capital account and can trade size. What do I mean by a large capital account size? I mean one hundred thousand or more dollars to start. This is really the only way you could make any real money by trading intraday and make a living at it.

The one thing I *can* tell you that works, is keeping it simple and it will be. I strictly am a position trader now. I made some money day trading and got out. I don't day trade anymore and I don't recommend you do either. I know you won't listen to me at least for now and you will day trade so just learn it the right way from the start if that's what you want to do.

The smart money is not your worst enemy in the market, although they are not trying to be your best friend either. They do however leave clues in the market that are up you to decipher and then act upon without hesitation or fear. Are they doing this to be nice to you? I doubt it! They just cannot hide some of the clues they leave. Once you know what you are looking for, you can take advantage of the clues and make a low risk, high reward entry into the market and have a high probability outcome.

Unfortunately, most retail investors and traders do not take advantage of these signals that the smart money leaves behind. They do a lot of damage to their accounts because of it. They actually try to do the opposite of what the smart money does, and end up on the wrong end of the market every time, thus causing themselves to lose money.

The smart money follows the path of least resistance to supply and demand areas. They show you the way. All you need to do is mimic their moves and you can make some money every day in the live markets. They can do all the heavy lifting, so why not just let them?

The professionals are only interested in making money and doing it by taking a longer term view. The smart money does not day trade. They have billion dollar super computers and code slinging geeks making a cool million a year for doing nothing but writing computer algorithms to tell the computer what to do, what to see and what trades to take.

As I said before all the smart money cares about is controlling their risk in the market and so should you! They are looking for a low risk, high reward high probability entry where their risk is controlled by how close their stop is to their entry. This is easy to state however very hard to execute in the live market for a retail investor and trader. Smart money is only looking for the highest probability outcome in the market, and again so should you!

Making money in the market today is really no different than how you make money in real life. An everyday example is when you go to the grocery store with a coupon to give you a discount on the product you desire to purchase. It's really no different in the market; you want to buy something on sale. Buy low, sell high.

We instinctively want to get the most value for our dollar. Why then would you want to buy when a stock's price is at its highest point in the live market? This is what retail investors and traders do every day. They wait and wait, then before they know it the price has had a big run up and they place an order out of anxiousness. Oopsy!

The problem is that retail investors and traders are conditioned to do just the opposite of this rule. They like *to think* they can buy low and sell high, however they have learned all of the wrong information which tells them to do the wrong thing from trading books and/or seminars. The books, seminars, and training that retail investors and traders put themselves through are often totally unrealistic in real world markets. Unfortunately, this often goes unrealized until it is too late most of the time.

Retail investors and traders buy and sell at the worst possible moments. When the price of an instrument has had a huge move up in price the retail trader is buying at the top of the move. When the price of something has had a huge move down in price they are selling at the very bottom. They have been taught to do this from the start and don't know any better.

Smart money is experts at buying at wholesale prices in the market, and selling at retail. In other words, buying low and selling high. Sounds fairly simple right? The Smart money is in the business to make money. Make no mistake about it; they are there to empty the retail investor and traders' account.

Once you to start to think like the smart money and adopt their mentality, you can see where they are selling or buying in the live market. Then you can make money right along with them instead of paying them. If you want to be consistently profitable in your investing and trading business, you *must* accept and absorb these basic principles. Buying at wholesale and selling higher at retail. Buy low sell high.

Buy waiting and buying high you have no one to pay *you*. By buying low everyone else who buys *after* you pays you. As I always say don't be the one who pays be the one who *gets* paid!

Learning to identify where the smart money is selling and buying on the price chart takes some time. Once you have this skill mastered, you will turn your trading around. I know I did. I had to unlearn 95% of what I had learned over the course of 4-5 years, however once I learned this new skill and started investing and trading with this understanding, I became consistently profitable almost overnight. Now I laugh all the way to the bank.

If you bought this book and have zero experience in the markets, I would encourage you study supply and demand investing and trading because it is the only method through which markets move from one value area to another. Look up supply and demand trading online and then watch and learn everything you possibly can. Become an expert at identifying where the smart money has their orders in the live market and then mimic their actions. Pretty soon, you will be laughing all the way to the bank as well.

When you make the decision to go live with real money, that's when it gets serious for you. You are now in competition with the big boys who have billions of dollars to play with and have the best technology in the world.

These professionals are pushing around billions of dollars on a daily basis to make the world work and make a profit to boot. If you think for one nanosecond that you will be able to out think, out trade, or out smart them I encourage too rethink that idea. Only one thing will happen if you go into the live markets with these people with this type of mentality and thinking. You will get FUBAR and then some.

Remember I said there are people in the market who will walk over dead bodies to get paid? I wasn't kidding. Hey listen they don't know you, care if you are having a bad day in the market and losing money to them. Matter fact they know what you as a retail trader are going to do before *you even* do it. Why? Because all retail traders work the same way and follow the same processes, look at the same charts and get the same training which we have said is all wrong from the start.

It is very easy for them to see the retail trader on the price chart because they are always making the same mistakes over and over and over again. They do it all day every day. Who do you think pays the smart money? Where do you think the smart money gains their profits from? I will tell you. It's *you*.

They *know* you are trading a scared money account and will make the same mistakes again and again. They *know* that you are your own worst enemy in the market not them. Do yourself a huge favor and get the right education and training from day one and you will have a chance at working with the best in the world.

I encourage you to study and use supply and demand trading. You can find a great supply and demand learning thread here: http://www.forexfactory.com/showthread.php?t=428204
Alfonso over there does an awesome job and goes above and beyond what any trader should do to teach new traders supply and demand trading. You should buy him a Ferrari when you become successful. Don't worry that it is a Forex related thread; supply and demand trading works on *any* liquid asset class on *any* time frame you chose to look at and trade from.

Go there and learn with the other new traders who are there. All the rules of using supply and demand for trading are listed on the first page of the thread on that forum. There plenty of chart examples as well so you can also learn chart reading there like I was talking about earlier in the book. You can also do a search online for a foundation and application course for supply and demand. They are online for *free* for anyone who can find the information.

The smart money leaves huge tracks in the market when they move price with their power and money. They can't hide this footprint they leave and it is your job to track them and then do what they are doing where they are doing it from. They take price to the areas where they want to get more orders filled at a certain price. See them and ride on their backs and make money along with them.

That is how I make money in the live markets every day. I just look for where the smart money have their resting orders and then wait for the retail sheeple of the herd to make their mistakes and buy or sell to or from them and then follow the smart money to where they are going to next. You don't need an MBA degree from a big fancy Ivy League college for that! Combine price action with supply and demand investing and trading and you have an edge over the retail sheeple of the herd.

Your job now as a professional investor and trader is to manage your money and control risk at *all* costs. You are basing all of the decisions you make on your developed logic—not with emotions. You are confident that you would much rather pursue a low risk entry than a small loss if it should happen. It is only low risk, high reward and high probability outcomes that you are looking for now, just like the Wall Street banks and the smart money.

Trading as a hobby will not work and only cost you money. Hobby and part-time investors and traders are rarely successful in this business. Ask yourself this question right now. Do any of my current hobbies make me money? Hobbies in general are entertainment that *cost* money and should you try to do trading as such it will be the most expensive hobby you ever took up and it will most likely *not* be fun. *At all*! Do not approach trading as a hobby. Treat it like a business. Develop a business plan, have goals, and understand what you want out of trading.

Every professional investor and trader I associate with treats investing and trading as a business and so should you. Having a plan to do your business is the most important aspect of making money in the investing and trading business especially when your real money is on the line in the live market. If you wish to be a consistently profitable investor and trader in today's live market and survive, build your plan to do so. Build your plan around what your intended goals are, the Wall Street banks do.

Investing and trading is a business. The business of making money with money and should be treated as such. In any business you have to work, whether you are the owner or you work for someone. You have to put in the time. It requires a great amount of time and mental stability to do it successfully and be consistently profitable on a daily basis. People trying to do it part-time are the ones paying those of us who do it for a business. Remember this because I talk about it a lot in my other books in a lot of the examples I give.

I recommend that if you are not able to give investing and trading your full-time attention, you should have your money managed by someone qualified who does it for a living. Learn as much as you can about the business, and then when you are ready, you can make the transition to doing it as a full-time business for yourself. You can certainly do the learning and education phase of this business part you time however you absolutely should not do the trading part of it part time.

How long does this learning take? There is no timetable set in stone. As someone new to this business it is critical you have all the information you need, and that you fully understand it and are able to act on it in the real-time live markets with real money. Going into the live markets and using your real money to invest and trade without educating yourself is like playing Russian roulette with a completely loaded revolver. Why would you do that to yourself?

The failure statistic of 97 percent is just about right. There are *many* reasons why brand new retail investors and traders fail. This book is going to give you some of the main reasons, and it will be up to you to take in this information and use it to your advantage to become successful. It will still be a long and hard road; however, if you can get your head around what this book says and then make every effort *not* to do these things, you have a good chance of having a positive outcome at your new business. You are going to be armed with what *not* to do. So as I said before *don't do it*!

There are no shortcuts to success in investing and trading. You will need to develop a "kill everyone" mentality to work in the live markets on a daily basis to be consistently profitable. You have to do the learning time if you want to drive the money train to the bank.

My final advice for beginners

The reality of the market is that there are people in there who are smarter than you, have waaaaaaaay more money than you, have better algo than you and are trying to take your money and transfer it from your account to theirs. They don't know you, care about you, or have any feelings if you lose. It's just business. The business of making money with money and it is always *your* money. Don't be *that* trader. Learn to do this business the right way from the beginning and you won't be.

Don't become one of the sheeple of the herd and do what everyone else is doing when and where they are doing it. The smart money can see this on the chart just like the sharks in the water and are looking to take advantage of the errors the sheeple of the herd make over and over again.

Who are the sheeple of the herd and who are the smart money you may be asking? The smart money is the Wall Street Banks, institutions, hedge funds, HFT's and dark pools. They are the liquidity providers and market makers. They are whom you need to be able to see on a price chart if you want to make money in the markets.

The sheeple of the herd as I call them are the unprepared or underprepared retail traders who are in the market without the proper training and education or psychological makeup who get FUBAR (fleeced up beyond account recovery) every day in the live markets. You also need to be able to see *them* on a price chart because you can also make money from *them* as well.

There are no shortcuts to success in investing and trading. You will need to develop a "kill everyone" mentality as I said to work in the live markets on a daily basis to be consistently profitable. You have to do the learning time and have your head on straight if you want to drive the money train.

Only do what you know to be true when working in the live market. The value areas are quite easy to spot once you have trained your eye to look at current price action and then look up and left. Spot them, draw your lines accordingly, then *wait* for PA to come back and fill your resting order you have waiting. If you are using an automated strategy which I *strongly* encourage you to do, all you will have to do is set it and forget it, sit back and wait to get paid. Finally the best advice I can give you is, always use a stop and **keep your hand off** that damn mouse!!

There are no short cuts and what I just said to study and learn can take quite a while. It all depends on you and how much time and effort you are willing to put in to learn what needs to be known to be a successful market participant. When you are learning and think you can skip something because it is boring you to learn it just think about your barbeque and those sharks with loaded revolvers waiting for you in the live market to come in unprepared and without a rule based plan.

The best advice I can give you is *not to enter* the live market with real money until you are ready. It's really that simple. No one is making you do this business. You are the boss and in control of what you are doing, *so have some*. Entering the live market and using real money before you are fully ready and confident enough to do so will only cause you to lose money and question your skills.

You should *already* have all the skills needed to be successful in the live markets *before* you enter. The people who are already in there are professionals who are ready to take advantage of new traders and take all their money. Don't be one of the sheeple of the herd.

It is not rocket science or neurosurgery being done in there. It is making money with money. Usually it is the smart money making their money with *your* money. Is that what you want? Do you want to keep making the same mistakes over and over again and paying the smart money and professional traders who *do get it*?

Trading in today's financial markets it is competition at the very top level, where the stakes are the highest. Educate yourself to be a competitor and a winner. You want to have success, right? You need to be prepared to work with the best market participants in the world. That's who are in there in the live Forex, futures and stock markets.

It is one thing to have a plan and practice it on demo it is however entirely another to execute it flawlessly in the live markets with your hard earned real money against the best market participants on the planet. Trading is global so make no mistake and think you are in there by yourself.

Having a plan and sticking to it is one thing that all investors and traders *must* overcome to be a successful market participant for a long term financial benefit. This should be the goal of anyone considering a business or career in the investing and trading business. Making *some* money every day should be the goal of all investors and traders no matter what asset class you are working in. This is easier said than done though.

Finally it is all about being organized and disciplined. Successful traders have this down pat. They have developed their trading edge over time and have mastered it and built their trading plan around this edge. Some of these traders even go as far as writing their plan out on paper and keeping it with them at all times.

It takes a lot of time and patience to develop this system and these investors and traders have taken the appropriate amount of time to get it down which in turn has made them into consistently profitable and successful market participants.

Learn not to make these mistakes detailed in this short book and you can become a consistently profitable market participant in no time. It takes a lot of hard work however if you are committed to doing this business then the amount of time it takes is not an issue. The market is always going to be there waiting for you. *ALWAYS*!

To really succeed at trading the financial markets, you need to not only *thoroughly* understand risk reward, position sizing, and risk amount per trade, you also need to consistently execute each of these aspects of money management in combination with a highly effective yet simple to understand trading strategy like price action and supply and demand principles.

Once you learn the core principles of how to trade with supply and demand you will rarely need to go back to reinforce anything. Everything is there for you right on the price chart in front of you. Once you have learned to quantify price action on a chart and then use that information to enter a position in the live market you will not need any other information.

Most futures traders spend many many hours looking for that magical combination of indicators that will reveal the "Holy grail" of winning trading strategies. They should *instead* be spending their time on learning what makes the market actually work which is supply and demand.

Concentrate on having on a solid well-constructed trading plan. The better your plan is, the more you're going to be able to move forward with confidence and zero fear.

Identify when your best trading schedule is. When do you find you do your best trading? During RTH, Asian session, London? If you can determine what time works best for you it can greatly help with your profitability. Only go in the live market you work in when the liquidity providers are providing liquidity.

The best traders *are the best* because they constantly try to improve themselves. I can't stress enough how important this mindset is in trading. The markets are dynamic, and they will demand the very best of you day in and day out.

There is really no easy way to do it honestly. There is a certain progression of steps *all* new traders must go through to be able to drive their own money train to the bank on a daily basis which I have detailed in the book. The progression of steps is to learn money management, gain a hold on your own psychology, learn to read the price charts of the instruments you choose to work in and finally learn how to quantify real supply and demand in the live market to make your trade decisions from.

There are no short cuts and what I just said to study and learn can take quite a while. It all depends on *you* and how much time and effort you are willing to put in to learn what needs to be known to be a successful market participant. For me it was days, nights, weekends and even some holidays. I just wanted to do it *that* bad. It takes a lot of dedication and time.

When you think you are going to try to shortcut it just remember there are sharks with fully loaded revolvers in the live market waiting for you to take that shortcut so they can take all your money.

Remember the smoke and flames coming out of your barbeque because you threw all your money in there and didn't have a rule based plan as to how to work in the live markets where you are in competition with sharks.

Brand new traders tend to self-sabotage their own efforts at the beginning of their trading careers and businesses because they had not learned that there is a lot to know and have mastered before one can become successful in this business. There are a lot of different things we can do to improve our trading, but there are also things we can do to sabotage our trading as well. One of those things is not getting or having enough information.

It is my goal in this book to give you the information that can help you right from the start of your new trading business the first day. It is so important for traders to start out right from the beginning because the outcome of not having done so is very expensive and no one likes to or wants to lose money. Unfortunately brand new investors and traders tend to lose almost all of their money on their first try in the markets.

I recommend you start off slow and build on success. You should study each part of what those new beginner series books talk about in detail separately and *master* each individual process before moving on to the next one. How long will that take? As long as it takes! There is no reason to be in any hurry because the market is there waiting to pay you some money every day.

As I said I like to think of it as a big ATM machine because it is open virtually 24 hours a day seven days a week just about. You just need to have the proper PIN# to get your money out. Do the training and education and do not make these mistakes in this book and you will be well on your way to having your own personal PIN# to make money in the live markets every day. It is all about putting all the probabilities in your favor to attain the lowest risk highest reward highest probability outcomes you can have in the live market when putting you hard earned money to work on a daily basis.

Oh and by the way. That big screen TV you paid the $1500 for at Sam's he bought for $900 marked it up and sold it to you for a tidy profit. When you are getting ready to execute that position in the live market think about the TV and ask yourself am I really buying at wholesale?

Bonus section

I put this bonus section in my new trader books because I feel it can help you get a huge head start. It took me years to find this information and now I give to you in this book as a bonus. You're welcome!

This bonus section is just a glimpse of what it is going to take to become successful in the live markets. If you are brand new to this business here are some ideas for using your time in the best way. You first obviously need to have a grasp on all of the data in the above sections. There is a lot of work to do and I hope this section can give you some ideas as to what you need to do.

Demo trading or simulated trading to get the practice of putting on a position and taking off a position is good. It is good for learning how to place your SL and PT and manage them if you work that way. Demo trading is very good to get to know how your software platform works and how to use all the tools it offers you. Drawing lines on your value areas, mapping PA etc.

If you don't have a lot of time right when you first get into this business to practice trading on demo during regular market sessions then what you can do is record the session and then trade it at a time when you can practice. I recommend that you get a trading platform that enables you to do this as it will help you to cut down your learning curve and practice time greatly. You want to be in there making *REAL* money don't you? Do what needs to be done and get it done!!!

I would like you to always remember that simulated/demo trading is just that. You are not trading against anyone so it does not really matter what you are doing. There is no one on other side of what you're doing. It is great for learning your chosen platform and learning your system/method. You do have a method or system and a rule based plan right? Remember on demo it's really about practicing your strategy and entries and exit's and *that's it*. It will not work the same in the live market so you should prepare yourself with that in mind.

Always remember that in the live market there *has* to be someone on the other side of your position to give it to you. I'll say that again. For every buyer there has to be a seller and for every seller there has to be a buyer, period. Keep in mind when there is someone on the other end of that position to have to give it to you in the live market they are trying to kill your account. It's how and the only way the market works. Hence Supply and Demand.

WHO is on the other side? If you have done your education properly and can see where the banks and institutions are on the price chart it's them and the retail trader who is have a realllllly bad day at that point and is making the huge mistake of buying or selling in an area of interest to the smart money where supply or demand is out of balance.

One mistake that new investors and traders make is that they get used to doing things in demo that they could *NEVER* do in the live real markets. We have all done it at one point when we were learning. In the live markets though this is where it starts to get real for you.

I recommend that while you are trading and learning in demo mode that you get all of the kooky stuff you want to try out of your system and have your fun in demo mode. Once you fund your real money capital account and go in the live market with real money you will have all that out of your system already.

Remember what I said above if anything else about the buyers and sellers. When you try all the kooky stuff you are doing on demo like trading 500 shares of xyz stock in the live market with your hard earned real money only one thing will happen. *YOU WILL LOSE ALL OF YOUR MONEY!!!*

Taking bad habits you develop into the live real money markets will get your account FUBAR in a hurry. I can only say at this point *DON'T DEVELOP BAD HABITS* to begin with and you will not have any problems. Traders develop bad habits in demo trading and then go in the live real money markets and wonder why are losing a lot of money and things are not working like they did on demo.

When you have had all your fun on demo and have then gotten serious and become consistently profitable on a daily basis for some time. I suggest taking a very small amount of money and go in the live market and take some positions and see if you have what it takes to do it live with real money. It's the only way you'll know. See if you really do have game as my mentor said to me. You can trade micro-cap stocks live in the market on a $500-$1000 dollar account size as long as you are trading small share sizes. This gives you an idea of what it like to experience the feelings of the live market both *good* and *bad*.

It's at this juncture I want to say that demo is *ONLY* good for applying entry and exit plans and should not be leaned on as a crutch. Demo trading isn't some video game. You will start to learn bad habits that will transfer to the live market and cause you to lose money and then you will be wondering what went wrong. What you can do on demo *YOU CANNOT DO* in the live real market and if you try to you will surely lose money. I can vouch for that first hand. Until you get serious *stay out* of the live market with real money.

I suggest you develop a morning routine. Get into the habit of doing the same thing every day all the time. Here is a good morning routine to start getting in the habit of doing every day before you go in the live market to work. Turn on your charts. While the charts are booting up review your journal and any notes you have made. OK charts are up. Look at current PA where is it in relation to the London and Asian sessions? Where is it in relation to the previous day's session? Now look above and left and below and left and see where current PA is. Where are the value areas? Where is the curve at? Draw your S&D value area lines accordingly, and then trade according to your plan.

How to find a mentor

I strongly recommend that any new trader tries to find a mentor if possible; a professional real money investor or trader who can answer questions from a real, live market perspective, someone who only invests and trades with real money. Experienced investors and traders can be of great value to the novice retail trader due to their knowledge base and their developed mental abilities to work in the markets full-time, using real money.

New investors and traders have a lack of psychological knowledge that in the beginning is a detriment to them, and they are their own worst enemy at this point. I would call or text my mentor and say I just did *this* or *that*, and he would just say, "In real money?"

I had doubled my demo account four months in a row on demo. Then instead of resetting it again, I let it go and took it up to over three hundred thousand dollars. Once I had done this, he urged me to go in the live market and see if I could really do it with real money. I finally went live and never looked back. I still have an occasional losing day now and then, though. No one is perfect. No one!

What I mean by a losing day is not making any money and giving the market some of my own money. That is my definition of a losing day. What's yours? I would rather eat broken glass and wash it down with gasoline than give the market any of my own capital.

I encourage you to get help even if you have to pay for it. The amount of time it can cut off your learning curve will be well worth the money spent, and the return on investment will be tenfold. It won't be inexpensive as most professionals are in the market and monitoring whatever positions they have and to mentor you means they need to take time away from what they need to be focused on so be prepared to pay if you want professional help.

The mentor I had and still call and ask questions to every now and then, trades a very large account and does very well. It is all he has ever done for a living all of his life. I did not have a mentor for live trading until I was already doing it and making some money consistently however as I said above if you can find someone who can help you from the start it will *greatly reduce* your learning curve.

As I said you are your own worst problem when you are just starting out in this business and a mentor can greatly help you from being a detriment to yourself and keep you from self-sabotaging your trading. To many times people come into this business with dollars signs rolling around in their eyes like some old cartoon.

As has been said before, this is not a get rich quick business unless you are a hedge fund, and using OPM (other people's money) and leverage or both. It is precisely the opposite for retail traders. It is a very slow growth of your equity curve and your business.

Don't get me wrong. You can and perhaps may make a lot of money in this business. Depending on the amount of capital you choose to deploy in the live market at any given time. The trader who mentored me is a full time trader who trades a very large account size. This business is all he has ever done for a living and the only "job" he has ever had. There are days where he pulls out five to ten thousand dollars or more. He is a former pit trader so he has firsthand knowledge.

Everything I have written in this book I have personally experienced from being in the trenches and battling the smart money for profits and I hope that once you read this whole book through the first time you will not have to go through what I did when I was first coming up and learning investing and trading.

I am self-taught and self-made and did it all on my own which makes the success all the sweeter. All of the businesses I own I have started on my own with no help or money from anyone. I just did it.

I never had a mentor until I was already trading live with real money. He would ask how I was doing and I would be cagy and answer "making a little" Interestingly he does not trade anything like I do. He is more of a quant than anything else. He likes his numbers. I do what the smart money is doing where they are doing it from and make my money along with them so should you.

Tips for the brand new beginner

http://www.informedtrades.com/index.php has a huge amount of free courses for the brand new investor and trader. Simit the owner over there has done a fine job at compiling all the data and information that a brand new investor and trader will need to know and can study there for free. You can journal there and also perhaps get your questions answered by other investors and traders to help you expedite your learning curve.

When I first started out, I went to a forum and got help from all the other traders there. It was an atmosphere of camaraderie and sometimes even a little fun competition. It made learning the markets fun. There are traders there from different walks of life with a common goal, and that is to learn to invest and trade in the markets.

I encourage you to find a forum where you fit in and to jump right into the fray and start learning. It is a great way to learn because members share all that they are doing so you can learn not only from your mistakes and triumphs but those of others, as well. It can be a fun way to learn. There are places to learn all types of trading on the Internet now. Find and pick one that best suits the style trading you have chosen to get into.

Here are some extra **tips** I can give you. If I have said it once I have said it 100 million times. Trade smart *OR JUST DON'T TRADE*! If you have to use margin or leverage you should not be investing or trading with real money as a beginner. Only invest or trade with money that is disposable and can't hurt you if you lose all of it.

When the market you are working is volatile take smaller positions. Always feel free to take your profit. The market is always going to be there with more. Only be in the market when the liquidity providers are there providing liquidity.

Do what the smart money does where they do it at and you have a much higher probability of a positive outcome. Trade what you see happening *NOT* what you *THINK* is *GOING* to happen. You can't lose any money in the market if you're *not in it*. Never ever enter a trend after it has begun. Never enter a position when the PA is sideways. Hence the CHOP SHOP.

If you don't really see an S&D level then hey guess what *don't enter*!! You don't have to always *be in* the market. If you just wait till PA gets to where you need it to be for you to get what you want. Let the market do all the heavy lifting for you.

Review every chart of every position you own – every day – even if you only allocate 10 seconds of eyeball time to each position.

All successful investors and traders I know have a daily pre-market routine. They all do the same thing to prepare for the market every day, the same way, all the time. They are in the habit of doing this every single day. They have a checklist of what their routine is and go down the list every day. They have their notes from their analysis right there so they can see them at a glance.

One of the reasons why professional traders have become successful is because they know what they are going to do before they take any action. It is one of the traits that all professionals I know have. They would not even think of going into the live market with their real money without having quantified what the price action of the asset they are working in is doing.

Build a watch list for equities. If you are investing and trading there are many different ways to trade equities. You have to decide what type of trader investor you want to be. Do you want to day trade intraday? I highly discourage this and it is the surest way to lose a lot of money. To day trade equities at most brokers you will need to deposit a minimum of 25 thousand dollars in order to trade intraday. Do you have twenty five large to blow?

You should create a watch list of stocks that are moving and fit your trading style. For those of you learning equities there is a cool and easy way to build a watch list and add stocks to your watch list if you use TOS charts. It goes like this: Plug in your metrics and do your scan on http://finviz.com. When the results come up go to the tickers tab and click on it. Right click your mouse high lite and drag it across the tickers. They are now on the clip board. Next go to your watch list(s) you made on TOS and click on the gear on the top of the watch list.

Next click on import and click the paste symbols from clip board button. The tickers you highlighted are now there in your watch list. If you build a TOS chart and link it by color to the watch list you can just use the up/down arrows on your keyboard to scan the list and analyze the charts for the symbols given in the scan from your metrics. It simple and easy and provides a lot of data to analyze for possible position purchases. Do this every night to build a nice trade able watch list.

BE CAREFUL once you have your list established to click the button that says "add to current symbols" or you will delete everything you have in there and replace them with whatever was on the clipboard.

You'll only make that mistake *once*. Trust me. Once the list is replaced you cannot get it back again. NOTE: The above directions only work with finviz scans as far as I know. That is the only way I have ever done it.

Hope this helps you in your investing and trading. Having a trade able watch list is the way to go making money with stocks. I trade my live real money account with Scottrade and watch my TOS charts in real time to monitor the positions.

You can get a free demo account on think or swim by just calling. Normally the feed is delayed by 15 minutes. I believe however if you call and ask the technical services person who answers the call you can get them to make it so your feed is in real time. This is important in the sense that if you need to make a real time decision to acquire a position the 15 minute delay could be a problem for that.

So there it is. You need to do your screen, develop a master watch list, transfer any possible candidates to a daily watch list, and trade it as long as it meets your criteria for entry. You should know what your profit margin and stop loss will be *before* you take a position.

If you want to know where the smart money is going to trade look on http://finviz.com. Go to groups at the top. Then click on charts. Then look at the right hand axis. It will be highlighted in yellow for you telling you what is the highest percentage. Click on the group chart and it will bring up all the symbols for it. Then just screen the group for your screening metrics and find a trade. There is always something you just have to know *HOW* and *WHERE* to look for the information

Here are a couple of capital scenarios for a beginning day trader or swing trader. You can begin to trade immediately in the live market with real on money on as little as $500. Once you have completed your training and education, become consistently profitable on demo and composed your rule based plan for the type of investing and trading you wish to do you can then begin to trade in the live markets with real money.

The only way to trade in real time in the live market with real money and do it on a $500 account size is to trade micro Forex or micro-cap stocks. Only these two types of instruments would allow you to get a taste of the live market with real money and see if everything you have done up to this point will actually work in real time live with real money. I recommend that all brand new investors and traders start out in this way due to the brutality and volatility of the markets. Brand new investors and traders have no idea what it will be like in the live market using their real money until they actually do it.

Model yourself repeatedly after highly successful traders – adopting both their attitudes and behaviors. Find a successful trader or investor or one of each and study them. Look at hedge fund owners who have returned 20% or more over a prolonged period of time. Study them then try to develop a style which emulates this successful method and make one of your own. Before you know it *YOU* will be the one making 20% or more in your business.

The absolute biggest advantage when it comes to being successful in investing and trading is having stuck with it. That's when you can feel good and know that no one did it but you. The more you try to find the Holy Grail and jump from method to method the less chance you will have to succeed in investing and trading. Hence the 97% failure rate. Those of us who *HAVE* made it and *ARE* successful have traveled a looooong road.

Keep a journal of your market activity

One of the most common traits all of the successful investors and traders I know is that they all use a journal. If you get into the practice of writing down all of your trades in a journal the information in there can be invaluable to you should you hit a rough patch of trading. Trust me everyone hits a rough patch at some point.

To become consistently profitable and successful in investing and trading can be a long and very expensive learning curve. To go from being a novice who makes a lot of mistakes to a professional who avoids making them like their life depended on it takes quite a bit of time. A journal can help cut down the time it takes and also help with the learning process everyone must go through.

You might think it takes too much time to journal all your trades however the time you take while doing it is what can be the greatest value of all. The more data you write down the better idea you can have of what is working and what did not work. The journal can and should be used as a self-education tool to further your trading career. I know of no successful professional investor or trader who has not used a journal. They only act on a position if the data points to having had a low risk high reward high probability outcome.

One of the first questions I ask anyone who comes to me for mentoring help is if they use a journal in their trading and if so how long they have been doing it. The information I can look at in the journal can help me to ascertain how I can help them right from the start. I can see their strengths, weaknesses and if they are biased toward any type of trading. I can also look at how they can improve their efficiency and make suggestions on other data they may add to their journal.

There are plenty of ways to journal trading activity and I offer a great template for free at my website as my way of saying thank you for purchasing this book. Please feel free to stop by any time and download it for your own personal journal. The template is fairly comprehensive however you may feel free to add to it as you see fit for your own personal style of investing and trading.

Being consistently profitable in this business is challenging to say the least however if you give yourself a winning edge you can be quite successful. One of the ways to do it is with the journal. In the journal you can put down the aspects of the positions you take that where positive and negative should you have the occasional loss.

In addition to the technical aspects of your trading you record in the journal you can also include how the market was acting, the sentiment, and what the conditions were that caused you to enter a position. Recording this type of data in your journal will give you a reference point to see what conditions you set that were met that gave you the highest probability for having a positive outcome in the market at that time.

Most investors and traders like to think they are very decisive and disciplined. Then they go back and read the notes in their journal and find out they made some mistakes and perhaps even may have deviated from their trading plan. This information can be a good thing in the sense that it will help to improve any problems which may be arising in the daily work in the market.

You must be able rationalize why you did things the way you did them when in the live market. You are in control of all the variables that enable you to have a positive outcome as a market participant. So have some control and journal why you did it a certain way. No one is making you do this business but you.

I always tell clients to think like they are a money manager of a hedge fund or mutual fund. I have them think about how they would explain their choice on entering a position to their client and what the client would think of their reasons to having their money entered into the live market in this manner. If you can't convince the client how do you convince yourself?

Once you have your desired template and the data which you would like to have in the journal you can go back and see your winning positions and then work to emulate those conditions in the future in the live market over and over again. Seeing what you did where and when you did it for a positive outcome can give you trading an edge that will last you forever.

Having a winning edge is what separates the consistently profitable investors and traders from the sheeple of the herd. When you can see what you did right and know what they are doing wrong you can capitalize on their mistakes and realize more profits.

Over time as your account balance builds up it will be just be a matter of adding more size to your positions when entering the same way you have been doing it all along on the winners. That's how serious money is made in the markets. If you have learned how to see where the supply and demand value areas are on the price chart this will only add to your edge and give you the confidence to enter with the smart money with zero fear.

Over the long run you will just develop the habits of taking a position without even thinking about it when your conditions are met in the market. The reason is because you have reviewed what works over and over again in the analysis you have done on your journal and know what works when and also more importantly what does not.

Another way that the journal can be of great assistance is in your morning routine. You do have a morning routine don't you? You can use the journal as a way to see what times in the market you have been working in that the liquidity providers are providing liquidity as that is the only time you should be in the market anyway.

You can tell where the supply and demand value areas are going to be because you have already mapped them out and recorded the data in the journal for future reference. It is these value areas that you want to be trading from and taking your profits at. You can even assign them a points system so that you can know when the best time to enter will be.

The best journals act as a way to improve one's investing and trading and thus profitability. That's what it's all about in there is making money and keeping it. If I have said it once I have said it one hundred million times. No one wants to lose $200-$300 on a 50-50 set up however if you have 4-5 trading days or months or years the $300 becomes immaterial because you were prepared for the best possible outcome. A journal can help you make those preparations.

Develop a set pre trading routine

It is all about identifying a big move, either up or down, and then looking to the left to see where it came from and how much time the price spent at that value area before it shifted. This is the first thing I do in the morning when I turn on my charts as part of my morning routine. I look at current price, look at the overnight price action, and see where price was in balance in the overnight session. I then just follow the current price action backwards to see the whole move.

I suggest you develop a morning routine. Get into the habit of doing the same thing every day all the time. Here is a good morning routine to start getting in the habit of doing every day before you go in the live market to work. Turn on your charts. While the charts are booting up review your journal and any notes you have made. OK charts are up. Look at current PA where is it in relation to the London and Asian sessions? Where is it in relation to the previous day's session? Now look above and left and below and left and see where current PA is. Where are the value areas? Where is the curve at? Draw your S&D value area lines accordingly, and then trade according to your plan.

You should focus on one market at a time and become an expert at it. This will enable you to make a very good living. A trader friend of mine said to me one time. "Why do you want to learn a bunch of markets when you can just add another contract to what you are already doing that is making you money"? It was like he punched me in the face. Talk about an AHHHA moment!!

I hope you have enjoyed this bonus section as it will serve you well if you follow the advice I give in here. No one wants to spend a lot of time doing all the education and training to do this business only to find that they lose money right away. Making a comfortable living from investing and trading the financial markets is completely possible if prepared for in the right manner.

If you start off small a build on success you will have a much better chance of having long term success and longevity in the business.

Oh and one last thing.

Don't stay long too long!

Extra links

Here is a great link with a lot of frequently asked questions by brand new traders and investors. http://education.howthemarketworks.com/stocks/beginner/practice-stock-trading-questions/ I encourage you to have a look and try to absorb a little bit of the basic information at a time. You don't need to know it all by heart verbatim however it can help you to understand some of the mechanics of how the markets work.

This link helps you to have a better understanding of how stocks are affected by supply and demand. http://www.investopedia.com/university/stocks/stocks4.asp

Frequently asked questions

Question: When would I be able to quit my job and trade full time?

Answer: To be very conservative and safe not before your income from your investing and trading matches what you make in your current employment.

Question: What kind of investor or trader should I be?

Answer: Figure out what is going to work best for your personality, lifestyle and capital you have to invest.

Question: What can I do to stack the odds in my favor?

Answer: Do the education time the right way from the first day. Use supply and demand and price action.

Question: How long will it take me to become consistently profitable?

Answer: It varies for everyone. It took me 5 years.

Question: What asset class is best to trade?

Answer: The one you see price action the best in and makes you the most money. This eBook is mainly about Forex though.

Question: How many asset classes should I trade?

Answer: I recommend no more than 3. The human brain can only process so much information at one time.

Question: How much time does it take be become consistently profitable?

Answer: That will depend on how fast you grasp the core principles of this type of supply and demand investing and trading

Question: What is the best time frame to invest and trade from?

Answer: I recommend using a daily chart however the method works on all time frames.

Question: What is the best asset class to use this method on?

Answer: That is the beauty of this type of method it works on any asset class. I like to use it for equities and have also used it for Forex futures, crude oil, gold and natural gas with very good results.

Question: How long does it take to fully know this method?

Answer: If you have no experience at all and are just starting out you can get it fairly easily. It took me about a year because I had to unlearn much of what I had previously learned.

Question: Do you use this in all of your investing and trading decisions?

Answer: Yes I do. I only make decisions based on my quantifying supply and demand and the chart.

Question: Does it work all the time?

Answer: Nothing works 100% of the time and to have that belief is a sure recipe for disaster.

Question: What kind of winning percentage will I have using this method?

Answer: You can actually lose quite a bit and still make a nice living using this method. That's what makes it so great.

Question: What would cause me to lose a trade?

Answer: Any number of mistakes however I have found that if I should take a loss it is most likely due to having seen the value area wrong.

Question: What are HFT and AMM?

Answer: HFT stands for high frequency trading and AMM stands for automated market maker. It is thought that about 70% of the market is traded by these computers now.

Question: Do you offer training in this style of investing and trading?

Answer: I offer private mentoring services for beginning investors and traders have are having problems grasping these methods. Feel free to contact me to find out what is required to get on my schedule.

Question: How long does it take to become consistently profitable enough to trade real money?

Answer: As long as it takes. I always tell my students that they do not need to be in any hurry because the market is always going to be there. There are 250 trading days in a year, so you have plenty of opportunities.

Question: Who is the best broker to use for a demo account?

Answer: I would pick a broker who can offer you a demo that you can practice on for a prolonged period of time. Meaning they will give you an unlimited time to learn to invest and trade on their demo.

Question: What is the bare minimum amount of money I can start trading with in the real markets?

Answer: You could start using as little as a hundred dollars if you were trading micro Forex. This gives you exposure to the live market and can also help you start to develop the psychology needed to move up to trading full lots with a bigger account size.

Question: Which is the best investing and trading forum to join?

Answer: I encourage you to check them all out and get a feel for the kind of investors and traders that are in there. Then choose one that matches your style of investing and trading.

Question: What are the best asset classes to invest and trade in?

Answer: You need to figure out what your goals are for your trading business to answer that. Do you want to make short-term income? Do you want to build up your account balance? Do you want to increase your wealth for the long-term? Figure this out before investing and trading real money.

Question: What is the best time to trade?

Answer: When the liquidity providers are providing liquidity.

Question: Who is the smart money?

Answer: Smart money is the banks, institutions, hedge funds, HFTs and black pools. They are the liquidity providers and market makers. They are whom you need to be able to see on a price chart if you want to make money in the markets.

Question: How do I start a journal?

Answer: You can start a journal at the forum where you are learning and also on your own. It can be a Word file, Excel file or just a plain Notepad file. You can also take screenshots of all your charts and save them to a picture file. Many traders post screenshots of their charts in the forums.

Question: How long did it take for you to feel comfortable working in the live markets with real money?

Answer: Five years.

Question: What markets do you work in?

Answer: I position trade equities and have my own Nano hedge fund. I also manage my own ROTH IRA money.

Disclaimer

This book is for educational purposes only. Futures, options, equities, and spot currency trading have large potential risk and traders should be well-educated before putting real money at risk. You must be aware of the risks and willing to accept them in order to invest in all markets. Never trade with money you can't afford to lose. This book is neither a recommendation, solicitation, nor an offer to buy/sell a futures contract or currency.

Forex, futures, stock, and options trading are not appropriate for everyone. There is a substantial risk of loss associated with trading these markets. Losses can and will occur. No system or methodology has ever been developed that can guarantee profits or ensure freedom from losses. No representation or implication is being made that using the trading concepts methodology or system or the information in this book will generate profits or ensure freedom from losses.

HYPOTHETICAL OR SIMULATED PERFORMANCE RESULTS HAVE CERTAIN LIMITATIONS. UNLIKE AN ACTUAL PERFORMANCE RECORD, SIMULATED RESULTS DO NOT REPRESENT ACTUAL TRADING. ALSO, SINCE THE TRADES HAVE NOT BEEN EXECUTED, THE RESULTS MAY HAVE UNDER-OR-OVER COMPENSATED FOR THE IMPACT, IF ANY, OF CERTAIN MARKET FACTORS, SUCH AS LACK OF LIQUIDITY. SIMULATED TRADING PROGRAMS IN GENERAL ARE ALSO SUBJECT TO THE FACT THAT THEY ARE DESIGNED WITH THE BENEFIT OF HINDSIGHT. NO REPRESENTATION IS BEING MADE

THAT ANY ACCOUNT WILL OR IS LIKELY TO ACHIEVE PROFIT OR LOSSES SIMILAR TO THOSE SHOWN.

Made in the USA
Middletown, DE
06 March 2015